MENSA
Secret
Codes
for Kids

ISBN 0-439-10842-X

Text and puzzle content copyright © 1995 & 1997 by British Mensa Limited.
Design and artwork copyright © 1995 & 1997 by Carlton Books Limited.
All rights reserved. Published by Scholastic Inc., 555 Broadway, New York, NY 10012, by arrangement with Carlton Books Limited.

12 11 10 9 8 7 6 5 4 3 2 1   9/9 0 1 2 3 4/0

Printed in the U.S.A.   01

First Scholastic printing, September 1999

MENSA
Secret
Codes
for Kids

Robert Allen

SCHOLASTIC INC.

New York Toronto London Auckland Sydney
Mexico City New Delhi Hong Kong

INTRODUCTION

A picture book that's really a treasure map . . . A message
to King Arthur in a mysterious code . . . Strange symbols
as a guide to getting out of a difficult maze . . . Can *you*
solve these very challenging puzzles? Codes are also fun.
In this collection of more than 100 exciting puzzles, you
will have a number of codes that at one time would have
carried life-or-death messages and that Mensa has turned
into puzzles. To help you there is a Spy School section
where you can learn how the codes are constructed and
how to crack them. With a little ingenuity, all these codes
can be cracked!

Good Luck and Have Fun!

How To Join
MENSA

If you like puzzles, than you'll like Mensa. It is the only club that lets you in just because you are good at puzzling. Mensa has 120,000 members throughout the world (with the majority in the U.S.A. and Great Britain). The great thing about Mensa is that you get to meet so many people with different interests. For more information about American Mensa, you can write to American Mensa Ltd., 1229 Corporate Drive West, Arlington, TX 76006-6103.

Sam Cody's Spy School

HI! I'M SAM CODY and before you try the puzzles in this book I'm going to send you to school. Don't worry, it's not the usual sort of school. This is my very own spy school and I'll be teaching you how to crack secret codes. The rest of the book will contain puzzles that help you test just how much you've learned.

Almost all the codes in the book will be taught in this section but, just to keep you on your toes, there are some puzzles where I've given you no clues at all and you'll have to work them out for yourselves.

WARNING
If you would rather try to crack our codes the hard way don't read on, but go to Page 14.

Let's try something easy first. There are some forms of disguised writing that are not really codes at all but they can still be used to convey secret messages. What do you make of this?

CAHE RWDO SAH TSI TTEERLS XIMDE PU

If you look closely you will see that this is just plain English with the letters rearranged. The message reads: "Each word has its letters mixed up."

There are plenty of other really simple forms of disguised writing. Here is another. It looks strange at first but you will soon see that there is only one small trick involved.

KUST DHANGE YHE BIRST OETTER PF DACH BORD

Double Dutch? No, the words are in plain English but the first letter of each has been replaced with a random letter. The message is: "Just change the first letter of each word." Once you have picked up a few tricks like this you can make up all sorts of secret messages. Try taking all the vowels out of your message like this:

MSSGS WTH N VWLS LK VRY STRNG NTL

Y GT TH KNCK F RDNG THM

You should quickly realize that this reads: "Messages with no vowels look very strange until you get the knack of reading them." Let's look at just one more simple trick before we get on to real codes.

What do you think this is all about?

SREDAER   LAUSAC   LOOF   LLIW

SDRAWKCAB GNITIRW

Stumped? The message is plain English written backwards. There are hundreds of variations on these tricks. Try removing the vowels *and* writing backward, for example. There are hundreds of different variations on these tricks. The only limit is your own ingenuity.

One of the simplest codes was invented by the Roman emperor Julius Caesar and is known as Caesar's Letter. To use this you need to make a code wheel. It consists of two wheels, one inside the other, with an alphabet written around the edge of each. Start off with all the letters on the outer wheel being next to the same letters on the inner wheel.

Sam Cody's Spy School

7

Sam Cody's Spy School

Now turn your inner wheel clockwise by just one letter. Already you have a secret code! Now instead of writing A you write B, instead of B you write C, and so on. Using this code a word like DOG would come out as EPH. By setting your wheel to different positions you can create 25 different codes. Try this example (the wheel has been turned so that J on the inner wheel is next to A on the outer):

HXD LJW ANJM CQRB FRCQ NJBN

Answer: "You can read this with ease."

Caesar's letter is what is called a 'substitution code' because it simply substitutes one letter for another. However, you don't have to use letters. How about trying numbers instead?

The very easiest sort of numerical substitution code involves giving letters a value based on their position in the alphabet. Using this code A=1, B=2 and so on until you reach Z=26. Now try working out what this means:

14.21.13.2.5.18.19/ 3.1.14/ 5.1.19.9.12.25/ 2.5/

3.8.1.14.7.5.4/ 9.14.20.15/ 12.5.20.20.5.18.19

"Numbers can easily be changed into letters," reads the message. When you have mastered the principle, you can start to work out variations. The obvious one is to number the alphabet backward.

On the other hand you could start in the middle and number the letters from M to A as 1 to 13, and N to Z as 26 to 14. Or you could give the first half of the alphabet odd numbers (A=1, B=3, C=5, etc) and the

second half would have the even numbers (N=2, O=4, P=6, etc). All you need is ingenuity.

Another type of code that can be a lot of fun is the grid. We have included three variations on this theme. The first is the simplest but it is also the most useful as it can be used both in writing and for flashing messages with a light or banging them out on the wall of your prison cell.

	1	2	3	4	5
A	A	B	C	D	E
B	F	G	H	I J	K
C	L	M	N	O	P
D	Q	R	S	T	U
E	V	W	X	Y	Z

In the diagram above, you will see that the letters have been written into a 5 x 5 grid (I and J share a space). You can now describe the letters by their coordinates. So instead of A you write A1, B becomes A2, and so on. If you wanted to use this code to beat out a message to a prisoner in the neighbouring cell you would use two sets of thumps with a short pause between them. Thus A would be thump-pause-thump and B would be thump-pause-thump/thump.

Sam Cody's Spy School

Try to decode this message just for practice.

E4.A5.D4/A1.C3.C4.D4.B3.A5.D2/E2.A1.E4/D4

C4/E2.D2.B4.D4.A5/D3.A5.A3.D2.A5.D4.C1.E4

Did you do it? It reads: "Yet another way to way to write secretly". But you are not finished with this code yet! Why not write the letters into the grid in a different order? Backwards, for example. It really doesn't matter what you do just so long as the person receiving your message knows how to decode it.

A mystical sect called the Rosicrucians are responsible for one of the most interesting grid codes ever devised. The trick with this one is to compose your message by leaving out the letters and drawing the relevant section of the grid. Since each section contains two letters you use the dots to indicate which one you mean.

A B	C D	E F	ST
G H	I J	K L	Y Z U V
M N	O P	Q R	W X

People being ingenious, they soon came up with a way to complicate the Rosicrucian grid even further. They altered the grid so that each segment except the last now contained three letters. Then they devised a different way of using dots to select the letters. If you showed a section of grid with no dots, then you were to select the first letter from the left. If you showed

one dot you took the second letter from the left. Two dots stood for the third letter from the left.

A B Ċ	D E Ḟ	G Ḣ İ
J K̇ L̈	M Ṅ Ö	P Q̇ Ṙ
S Ṫ Ü	V Ẇ Ẍ	Y Ż

Take a look at these messages and see if you can decode them. One uses the basic Rosicrucian code and the other the more elaborate version:

⊐<⊏⊔L⊏ ⊐⊓∨∨
L⊓<⊡ ⊐⊐⊔
<⊐⊐⊐∨<⊏⊐⊡

⊐L⊔ ⊏⊐⊐⊐ ⊐L⊔⊡
⊔⊡⊐

Message 1 reads:
  "Murder most foul and unnatural." (basic)
Message 2 says:
  "The plot thickens." (more elaborate)

There are many other forms of coded writing that involve substituting symbols for letters. One of the most interesting was a system that used mystic symbols based on the names of the planets. This was

Sam Cody's Spy School

favored by alchemists who feared that their secret discoveries would be uncovered by a rival. The code would not keep an experienced agent at bay for very long but would outwit most parents and teachers nicely. As it is decorative you could use it for including secret messages within a drawing.

A	B	C	D	E	F
☉	♃	♄	♆	♅	♁
G	**H**	**I**	**J**	**K**	**L**
♀	♂	☿	☾	♉	♊
M	**N**	**O**	**P**	**Q**	**R**
♋	♌	♍	♎	♏	♐
S	**T**	**U**	**V**	**W**	**X**
♑	♓	♈	♒	➣	X
Y	**Z**				
Y	Z				

Here is an example for you to work on.

☉♆♆ ♋♅♐♄♈♐Y ☉♌♆
♓♍☉♆♑ ♃♊♍♍♆ ♓♍ ♓♂♅
♃♐♅➣

The message reads: "Add mercury and toad's blood to the brew."

Morse code, invented by Samuel Morse who telegraphed his first message in 1838, has been widely used to transmit secret information. In the World War II it was a vital aid to members of the resistance who needed to keep in touch with the Allies. Its system of dots and dashes makes it one of the most adaptable codes in common use.

A	B	C	D	E	F
·—	—···	—·—·	—··	·	··—·

G	H	I	J	K	L
——·	····	··	·———	—·—	·—··

M	N	O	P	Q	R
——	—·	———	·——·	——·—	·—·

S	T	U	V	W	X
···	—	··—	···—	·——	—··—

Y	Z
—·——	——··

You can send Morse messages very rapidly by radio, telegraph, flashing lights, sounds, and many other ingenious methods. The code takes very little time to learn (though transmitting and reading at speed are skills that do take time to acquire).

As with other codes it is possible to make changes that will fool an outsider who gets hold of your message. For example, you can exchange dots for dashes and vice versa.

Sam Cody's Spy School

13

Here is a Morse code message for you to try:

■••• ••■ ■ ■•■• ••••

■•■• •■ ••• ••• •• ■•• ■•■■

••• •■■• ■■■ ■ ■ • ■•• •• ■•

■ ••• ■•■• ••• ■■■ ■•

•■•• •■ ••• ■

■■ ■■■ ■•• ■•• •■ ■•■■

The message reads: "Butch Cassidy spotted in Tucson last Monday."

Another very commonly used code is semaphore, which depends on the sender using flags held at varying angles to represent letters.

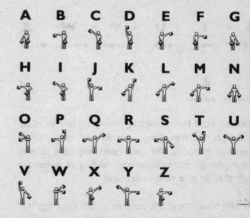

The usefulness of semaphore is limited for practical purposes by the fact that the sender needs to be in

Sam Cody's Spy School

plain sight of the recipient. This is not a bad way of, for example, sending a message from one ship to another but it is not nearly adaptable enough for espionage work. What does this semaphore message say?

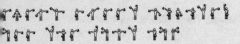

Message reads: "Enemy fleet sighted off the port bow."

Braille, the system of writing devised for blind people, can also be used as an effective code.

A	B	C	D	E	F
G	H	I	J	K	L
M	N	O	P	Q	R
S	T	U	V	W	X
Y	Z				

A system of dots based on a domino layout will allow you to write a message that only initiates will be able

Sam Cody's Spy School

to decode. Look out for dots in our puzzles – not all of them are written on dominoes!

Try this message for practice:

⠃⠗⠁⠊⠇⠇⠑ ⠓⠑⠇⠏⠎ ⠞⠓⠑ ⠃⠇⠊⠝⠙

Message reads: "Braille helps the blind."

You can devise symbols of your own to represent letters. Here is a system using differently divided circles.

A	**B**	**C**	**D**	**E**	**F**
⊙	⊘	⊖	⊘	⊗	⊕

G	**H**	**I**	**J**	**K**	**L**
⊕	⊖	⊖	⊘	⊕	⊖

M	**N**	**O**	**P**	**Q**	**R**
⊕	⊖	⊕	⊕	⊕	⊖

S	**T**	**U**	**V**	**W**	**X**
⊗	⊗	⊗	⊗	⊗	⊗

Y	**Z**
⊗	⊗

Here is a message using the circle code:

⊙   ⊖⊖⊖⊕⊗⊘⊖⊖   ⊕⊕⊗⊗⊗
⊗⊕   ⊘⊘⊖⊘⊗⊕⊗⊖⊘⊖⊖⊖⊕

Message reads: "A circular route to understanding."

Finally, here is another code system that was developed for use by the blind. It is called Moon writing after its inventor William Moon.

Sam Cody's Spy School

A	B	C	D	E	F
∧	∟	(	)	⌈	⌠

G	H	I	J	K	L
⌐	⊙	I	<	⌊	L

M	N	O	P	Q	R
⊥	N	O	⌐	⌐	⟍

S	T	U	V	W	X
/	⊥	∪	∨	∪	∩

Y	Z				
⌐	Z				

Just like Braille it was intended to be embossed on paper so that a blind person could read it by feeling the bumps with his fingertips.

Here is a Moon message:

⌐O∪ ∩ILL I⌐ O∨⌐\
⊥⌐⌐ ⌐OON ∩O⊥∩ ⌐O∪
\⌈∧) ⊥⊙\/

Message reads: "You will be over the moon when you read this."

Now you have enough codes to solve all the puzzles in the book. Remember we have sometimes made things just a bit harder by adding variations to the original code. You will need to be on the lookout for tricks and traps.

Sam Cody's Spy School

Templar trouble

The mysterious sect of the Knights Templar guards a dread secret. For centuries their members have protected this vital information from prying eyes. However, just one record of their secret exists in written form. You have discovered what you believe is a reference to it in an old book. However, the exact location has been cunningly encoded. Can you work it out?

Answer Number 28

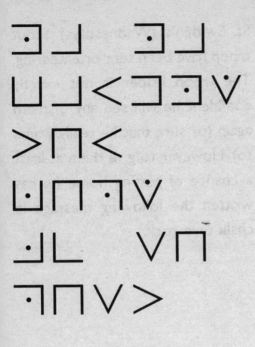

Templar trouble

Scout cipher

St. Swithin's (Wednesdays) Scout troop have been sent orienteering. The troop leader is not exactly confident he will see any of them again (or sure that he really wants to). However, to give them at least a chance of getting home he has written the following message in chalk on a rock.

Scout cipher

Trunk test

A trunk containing various anonymous long-lost manuscripts is unearthed in the middle of a farmer's field. Literary experts spend hours toiling over who the author was, but remain completely stumped. A son of one of the experts wanders over to the trunk and absent-mindedly runs his fingers over the mysterious pattern on the lid. His mother is startled when he cries out, "I know the author!" Do you?

Trunk test

Confusing cans

Sam went shopping with her bargain-hunting aunt one Saturday morning. They stopped by a basket full of reduced-price cans which had lost their labels, and only had what appeared to be illegible script on their bases. Sam studied the can her aunt had selected and carefully predicted what it would contain. Can you?

4☉◯♄♀

4♄☉●♌

Professor Potts was excavating a Roman villa when he came across a secret room. He guessed that this might have been a secret gathering place for Christians and when he saw this writing on the wall he was sure his theory was correct. What does it say?

Sam Cody reminds you that the Romans used letters as numbers!

P A 10 5-

O B 1 S 100-

U 1000

Romans rumbled

Teacher's travels

Class 2B arrive for a history lesson only to discover, to their intense delight, that their teacher, Mr Dullingham, is not at school. However, there is a large message written on the board. They study it with curiosity. Some of the children start to scribble on scraps of paper and then, after while, they begin to leave the room one by one. What is going on?

U TMHQ NQQZ
OMXXQP MIMK
AZ GDSQZF
NGEUZQEE.
MZKAZQ ITA
OMZ PQOAPQ
FTUE YMK SA
TAYQ QMDXK.

Teacher's travels

Fishy findings

Peter Whiting loved to go diving around old wrecks in Highsea Bay. One day, while he was on one of his dives, he came across an old treasure chest buried inside one of the wrecks. The chest was empty but written on the inside of the lid was what seemed to be a foreign language. Peter was intrigued so he brought it up to his boat and began to examine it. Soon he knew the truth and headed straight for shore.

What had he discovered? Here is the inscription.

Fishy findings

SQDZRTQD

HR ATQHDC

HM BZUD ZS

AZRD NE

GHFGRDZ

AZX BKHEER

Baffling bard

Janet was going to be in a Shakespeare play at her school. The whole of her family were going to see it but she wouldn't tell them which play it was. However, the family kept on asking her so frequently until finally, in exasperation, she wrote down the last two lines of the play in code and told them that if they could decipher the code, they would know immediately which play it came from. Can you work it out?

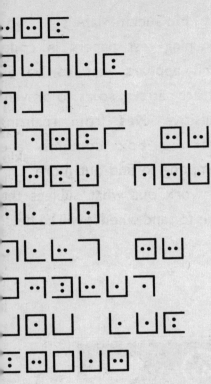

Baffling bard

The test is yet to come

Miss McGuckin labels a box containing test papers in code which appears just to be an abstract pattern, so as to prevent inquisitive eyes from realizing what the box contains, and attempting to find out more. Can you work out what subject the test is for, and when it will be held?

ζ ζγ ζζζ γ ζ

ζγζ

ζζζζ ζζ ζζζ γ

γγγ ζγζ γζγγ

γ ζ ζζζ γ

The test is yet to come

Missing Magnus

Magnus Loot, the newspaper tycoon, couldn't stand the pressure of work one more day. He decided to slip out of the country for a quick break. Naturally he couldn't tell anyone he was going or he would be bombarded with messages the whole time he was away. On the other hand if he were just to disappear there would be a panic to find him. Then he hit upon a plan. He would leave a coded message — not too difficult, just enough to keep them guessing while he made his getaway. This is what his secretary found on his desk:

Missing Magnus

ONEGO-THUOT-SFOEN-CRAFC-ABKRI-FYAD

Can you work out what Magnus was saying? The code is not at all clever, just a bit mixed up.

Hidden treasure

A glossy picture book is published and creates a great stir as it claims to lead the way to a valuable gold casket covered in diamonds. The race is on to decipher the code which leads to the treasure. Do you know where it can be found.

Hidden treasure

The Card clue

Sean received what he believed to be an anonymous Valentine's card, but when he looked at the picture more closely, he discovered a series of symbols which did not seem to fit in with the general design of the card. When one of his friends came round, Sean showed him the card, and was astonished when his friend declared who his secret admirer was. Can you?

Card clue

Muddled matrix

Jeff's dad had some slight frictio
with the tax people over a
unpaid bill and had to leave th
country rather suddenly. He lef
his son this note so that he woul
be able to follow as soon as h
was able. At first Jeff thought i
was a fiendishly cunning code bu
after hours of brain ache, h
realized that it wasn't a code at all
It gave his father's route quit
plainly! But you have to know
where to start.

Answer Number 8

A	P	O	R	E	U	S
G	H	E	N	S	K	A
N	T	D	A	M	F	R
I	A	R	A	M	R	A
S	T	E	T	S	A	C
K	R	U	F	K	N	H
O	K	G	N	A	B	I

Muddled matrix

Et tu Brute?

Brutus and his fellow conspirators have decided that they have had enough of Julius Caesar. In fact they have clubbed together and bought him a one-way ticket across the River Styx. Brutus has written to Cassius giving him details of their murderous plan. Rather stupidly he has used Caesar's own code (it is the only one he knows). Caesar's agents have obtained a copy of the message. Can you help them crack the code in time?

Answer Number 18

FN
BQJUU
BCJK QRV
RW CQN
OXADV

Et tu Brute?

Computer crime

Clive Kilobyte, inventor and computer software manufacturer, was disturbed to find that some of his best commercial secrets were being peddled to his competitors. But how? For weeks he kept watch without discovering anything. Then one day, quite by chance, he spotted a delivery note that was due to be sent out with a new batch of software. The numbers on the docket looked odd. Could they be a code? He tried 1=A but got nowhere. Then suddenly a thought struck him and within minutes he was able to summon the culprit and fire him on the spot. What was the secret?

Answer Number 15

19.22/19.26.8/26/13.22.4/
11.9.12.20.9.26.14/26.15.1
4.12.8.7/21.18

13.18.8.19.22.23/18/4.18.1
5.15/8.22.13.23/2.12.6/23.
22.7.26.18.15.8

26.8.26.11/8.26.14

Computer crime

Desert dilemma

You have been wandering through the desert for days and are desperate for water. Suddenly, on the ground you spot four casks that look as if they contain water, but beware, for these casks have been put there by the ancient people of the desert who only reward those who can crack their codes. Those who fail to do so are punished with death. On the outside of each of the four casks is the code. Can you work out which cask is safe to drink from before you perish in the scorching sun?

Desert dilemma

1. ⌴⌴ ⌐⌐ ⌐⌐·⌐
   ⌐⌐ ⌐ ⌐·⌴⊡

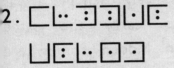

2. ⌐⌐·· ⊡⊡⌴⊡
   ⌴⊡⌴·· ⊡ ·

3. ⌐⌐ ⌐·⌴⊡
   ·· ⌴ ⊡··⌴⌴·

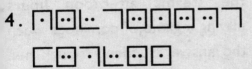

4. ⌐⊡⌴·· ⌐⊡⊡⊡·· ⌐
   ⌐⊡⌐ ⌐⌐·· ⊡⊡·

47

Dotty digging

For many years archaeologists had admired the exquisite pottery of the Rohoha tribe who had once lived deep in the Amazonian rain forest. Strangely each piece was found to carry the same inscription hidden somewhere within the pattern. What could it mean? Could it be the name of one of their gods, or perhaps some magical formula? No one could decide. Then one day young Dr Marissa Potts was idling away the steamy afternoon hours playing a game of dominoes when the answer suddenly struck her. Can you work it out?

Answer Number 59

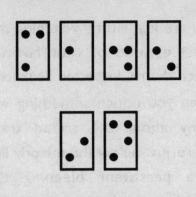

Bookham's blues

You are just sitting watching the latest episode of your favorite police drama, *Inspector Bookham*, when you notice something very funny about the sound track. There, just below the melody line, is a persistent bleeping that sounds just like Morse code. You quickly jot down as much as you can and then try to decode the message. This is the partial message you have:

Bookham's blues

− ···· −−− ·· −− −·· ····· −

·−·· −−− ··· ·− ···

−·· · ···· · ·−· −−· ·− −−·· ·

··− −··− − ····· ·

−− ··· ·−·

−··· · ·−·· · ···

·· ··· −− ···· · −−−− ·−·· −·−·−·−·

·−·· ·− −··· ·−· ·−·−· ·· −−·

− ···· · ·−·· · −·· ···· ·−··

Much Morsing

Ann Tenna is a radio freak. She spends all her spare time up in her bedroom surfing the airwaves. One day she comes across a very strange transmission indeed. Is this someone's idea of a joke, or is it a national disaster? See what you think.

Much Morsing

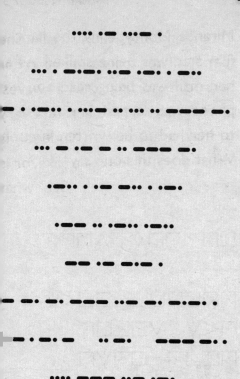

Filmstar frights

Miranda Moneypenny, the famous
film star, was being stalked. As al
her mail was being read and her
phone was tapped, any messages
to her had to be written in code.
What does this one say?

⌐⊔⊓ ⊓⊓⋁ ∧⊓⌐⌐>

⊓⊓⊏⊐⊔⌐ ⊐⊔<⌐

⊓<⋁ ⋁⊐∟⊐⌐

⊓⊏⌐⊓ ⊓⊓⋁⊓

⊔⊔⋁⊐⊓⊓ ⊐⊓⊔

⋁⊐∟ ⊔<⊏⊓⌐⊐⋁

⊐⋁ ⊔⊓⊓<⋁ ⋁⊓

⊐∟ ⊔⊔<⊐⊐⋁

54

Bolted boxes

A local business has a collection of top secret files, all individually labelled in padlocked boxes. To make the theft of any of them troublesome, each label is coded with the subject matter of each document. However one box has been tampered with. According to the code, what does the box contain?

Dad in danger

Agent Mucho Macho was on a mission of almost unimaginable danger when he received a message from HQ to say that he had at last become a father. Unable to break the cautious habits of a lifetime he asked his superiors to send his wife this message in code.

OBOE   VEER

MONO   OMEN

SHIN   EYED

BULB   ALLY

DEED   ACTS

KEYS   IBIS

Dad in danger

Party pooper

Alec Smart decided that he only wanted really clever children like himself at his birthday party. He sent everyone an invitation but put it in code so that only the brightest would know where to go. Unfortunately the code was not as hard to crack as Alec thought. He ended up with 36 guests who had a great time but wouldn't let him join in anything. See if you could have gone to the party. Once you know where to start it's easy.

Sam Cody says that once you get right to the bottom of the puzzle just follow letters that will make words. Beware – sometimes they are spirals, stripes or zigzags. The puzzle may start anywhere.

P	A	W	T	C	O	D	A	E	N
Y	R	O	H	U	M	N	Y	V	E
M	T	L	E	O	E	O	A	T	S
O	Y	L	T	Y	T	M	E	C	A
T	I	O	R	R	O	M	Y	P	L
E	F	F	A	O	F	T	F	E	L
M	Y	O	I	L	I	H	A	V	E
O	O	T	H	G	U	O	N	E	T
C	U	A	R	E	B	R	I	G	H
Y	L	N	O	N	A	C	U	O	Y

Party pooper

59

Generation game

Sam was exploring his grandfather's attic when he came across an old piece of slate with some strange symbols written on it in chalk. He showed it to his grandfather who, after studying it for a while, began to chuckle. He explained to Sam that it was a coded message and part of a game he used to play when he was a child. Can you work out what it says?

Answer Number 30

Generation game

Famous last words

Despite being a reformed character, when Ebenezer Scrooge finally died he couldn't resist making it hard for his relatives to get their hands on his wealth. He hid the money and left them this note. Can you work out where the treasure lies hidden?

KXXL
RXDNX
XHT DLX
KXX XXRT
NX YM
NXDRXG

Famous last words

Abducted astronaut

Major Mike McQuaid, one of NASA's top astronauts, has been abducted by agents of a foreign power. Days later FBI agents are handed a scrap of paper that a small boy saw thrown from a car speeding from the scene of the kidnap. There is a strange message that appears to be in some sort of number substitution code. They try all the obvious substitutions with no success. Obviously this one is something sneaky. Can you succeed where even the FBI have failed? You might find yourself in the middle of a mystery (hint, hint).

24.18.10.1.14/13.
26.6.18.1/13.3/1
1.18.22.9.18.13/
12.10.20.18.3.15.1
3/10.1/11.26.1.1
3.26/2.3.1.10.22.
26/4.26

Abducted astronaut

A rafty revelation

A group of teenagers built themselves a raft during an adventure holiday, and set off excitedly to sail on the huge lake nearby. After several hours on the water, they realized that they had drifted away from their camp, and had no idea how to get back. One lad suddenly noticed movement on the shoreline, and realized that their attention was sought. More movements followed with what appeared to be flags, and the route home suddenly became clear. What message did they receive?

A rafty revelation

Bridging the gap

You are travelling on foot through treacherously rocky terrain when you are confronted with a great, wide canyon – so deep that you can scarcely see the floor of it – which you must cross if you are to go any further. Spanning the canyon are three rope bridges. You must decide which bridge to take, but be careful because choose the wrong one and could find yourself dashed to pieces on the floor of the canyon. Beside each bridge is a coded sign which when decoded, may give you a clue as to which bridge to risk your life on.

Answer Number 34

1.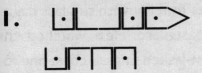

2.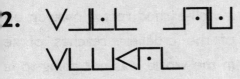

3.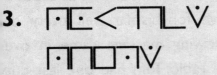

Bridging the gap

Shipping shocker

It was Tom Penwithick's last day a
a Coastguard. He'd watched the
storm-lashed English coast line fo
over 40 years and now it was time
to hang up his binoculars and take
a well-earned rest. However, one
of the cruellest reaches of sea
in the world was not going to le
him go without a goodbye to
remember. Just as he was about to
leave for his farewell party the
following message came in over
the radio. Tom had one last duty
to perform!

Answer Number 51

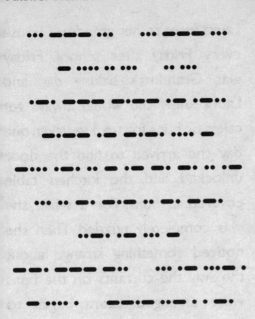

Bun bonanza

Laura went to her grandma's house every Friday after school. Friday was Grandma's baking day and Laura knew she would always get cakes or buns for tea. However, one day she arrived to find the door unlocked and the kitchen table covered in buns. For a while she was completely puzzled. Then she noticed something strange about the way the currants on the buns were arranged. Laura began to suspect that this was one of Grandma's little pranks. See if you can share the joke.

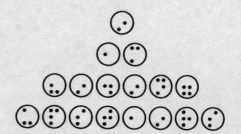

On a dank and dismal night, computer hackers break into Computer Craze headquarters in an attempt to find documentary details of the code they have been unable, as yet, to discover. They raid the offices and find a curious pattern imprinted on an imposing piece of card. Realizing its importance, they study it for hours to unlock the mystery of the computer code. What is it?

Hackers' horror

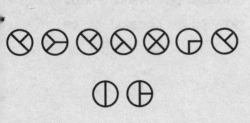

Shakespeare shocker

Professor V. Smart has a pet theory that Shakespeare's plays were in fact written by one Albert Grunge, a carpenter who used to live in the same street as Will. After years of campaigning Smart gets permission to open Shakespeare's tomb in search of clues. Among the dust and bones he finds a parchment which appears to be in some sort of code. Eventually he unravels the message but what he finds brings a glow to his cheeks!

Shakespeare shocker

Nautical numbers

Captain Routeless received an urgent radio message as he was navigating his ship through stormy waters early one morning. He thought there was interference on the radio as he listened intently to the message, but then realized that the letters were being spelt in the form of a number code easy to detect – the noise of the storm hindered attempts to understand human voices. What message do the numbers spell out?

122 12 121 21 11 21
221

11 2121 1 2111 1 121
221

1211 222 222 22 11 21
221

Answer Number 77

Rosie discovers a shopping list her mother has written, but the first item had been written in code. She thinks her mother is buying her a surprise for doing well in recent exams, and is anxious to discover what it could be. However, once Rosie has managed to decipher the code, her excitement quickly disappears. Do you know why?

Shopping strain

Strange last words

Colonel Strange of the US Cavalry is under attack from an enormous Mexican force led by General Sanguinario. Under cover of dark, he smuggles out a messenger carrying a coded plea for help. However, time is short. Unless you can unravel the code, Strange and his men are lost. Get cracking!

Answer Number 40

L	E	L	L	D	U	O	R	A	W
E	B	A	P	Y	A	N	R	E	E
S	R	A	S	D	O	B	D	R	S
S	A	E	L	E	E	U	D	E	U
L	O	S	I	I	S	R	T	N	D
E	B	O	T	N	A	E	E	N	A
S	C	I	N	N	F	V	N	B	U
T	L	O	S	A	E	O	A	D	M
G	R	E	L	S	S	M	R	L	A
E	N	A	N	O	O	P	E	C	L

Strange last words

Gang greetings

Jodie has been trying for months to join her brother's gang but they keep saying she's too young. At last she receives a coded note and she's pretty sure she knows who it's from. But what does it say? Is it good news or bad? Help her find out.

>⊓< ⊔⊐⊓

·⊐⊓⊐⊓ ⊓<⌐

⊐⊔⊏ ⊔∨

∨⊓⊓⊐ ⊔∨

>⊓< ⊔⊐⊓

·⌐⊔⊔·

∨⊐∪∨ ⊐⊓∨⊔

Gang greetings

Image problem

Katie has had a note from a anonymous admirer. Who can be? She rather hopes the writer Rick (tall, handsome and so co he's almost blue) but has a nast feeling it might be Stuart (fa spotty, nerd). Unfortunately th note seems to be in some sort code. Katie has puzzled over it a night but cannot work out what says. Then suddenly, whils brushing her teeth, it all become clear and Katie, though feelin slightly foolish, has a good laugh What did the note say?

Image problem

Dear Katie, Bet you thought
this was from lover-boy
Rick! Did you spend hours in
eager anticipation? Sorry to
disappoint you. It was only
from your best friend in all
the world (who you now now
Kate), Rachel.

Corruptive campaign

Snowbridge High School was having student council elections and party rivalry was rife. One day, one party's set of notes detailing their election campaign was missing. No one could find them until this short letter was found on the floor. After studying it for a while, the notes were recovered and the people responsible were dealt with. What does the letter say?

C2 A1 D4 D4

C3 C4 D4 A5 D3 / A1 D2 A5 /
C4 C3 / D4 C4 C5 / B1 C1 C4
C4 D2 / C4 B1 / D3 A3 B4 A5
C3 A3 A5 / A2 C1 C4 A3 B5 /
B4 C3 / C1 C4 A3 B5 A5 D2 /
C4 C3 / D3 A5 A3 C4 C3 A4 /
D2 C4 E2 / A4 C4 E2 C3 / A1
C3 A4 / D4 B3 B4 D2 A4 / B1
D2 C4 C2 / D2 B4 B2 B3 D4

B1 D2 C4 C2

D3 B4 C2 C4 C3

Corruptive campaign

Dotty Dave

The Daily Bugle started a Dotty Dave competition. All you had to do was spot a man called Dotty Dave carrying a copy of the Bugle, challenge him correctly with the words, "You are Dotty Dave of the Daily Bugle" and you would win £100,000. But how would you recognize him? Ah! That was the catch. The newspaper insisted that it had given all the information needed, but for weeks no one could work it out. Then, sitting on a train with her mum, young Georgina had a bright idea. She leapt up and challenged the man sitting opposite. Her mum, who had been cringing with embarrassment, was even more surprised when her daughter won.

ook at the picture and see how
he did it.

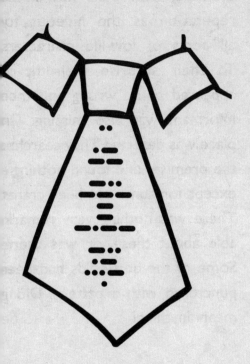

Dotty Dave

Crate clue

The police descended in force on the Dirty Duck, a bar with an evil reputation as the hideout for all sorts of low-life characters. To their surprise their tip-off appeared to be wrong and their informant was also missing. The place was deserted. They searched the premises and found nothing – except for some old beer crates. There was nothing very remarkable about these, or was there? Some of the bottle lids had been punctured with a pattern. Did it mean anything?

Crate clue

Wooden wonder

Sally buys a bargain do-it-yourself kit to make a smart desk unit. When she reaches for the instructions, she finds that they're written in an obscure language of which she has no knowledge. However, she finds a series of universal symbols at the bottom of the sheet, and is finally able to work out what to do. What do these instructions say?

Answer Number 82

Wooden wonder

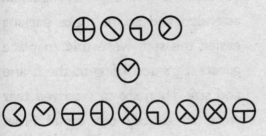

Catastrophic car park

Sir David Dunethwaite was holding a cocktail party at his huge mansion to celebrate his latest business success. Hundreds of people attended and so, to make parking easier, the staff were told to place guests' cars according to the brand and size. Then six cars arrived that were all exactly the same! How were they going to give the right car back to the right owner? There is a way to do it but, in order to work it out, you must study the registration numbers very closely.

A) Edward   1) B144 SFX

B) Steven   2) T113 VFM

C) Andrew   3) B147 FMB

D) Samuel   4) F423 BSE

E) Thomas   5) T205 WFO

F) Angela   6) U815 NBT

Catastrophic car park

Teacher torture

Miss Prim caught Becky passing a note to Clare during a Latin lesson.

"And what is this all about?" she enquired acidly.

"It's a note, Miss," replied Becky, helpfully.

"I can see that, but it's in some sort of silly code. What does it say?"

"It's not in code at all, Miss. Can't you read it?"

Miss Prim took a careful look at the offending note and quickly realized she couldn't unravel the message. Can you?

A L E T A H I
T A F N D E R
I T T A G G &
N E E L O R C
L E R O F V O
E M S O O B L
T S C H R A A

Teacher torture

Brick bother

Bill the builder is working on a new, top-security building used to store vast sums of cash and important documents for a famous company. He has access to the plans of the building, and is approached by Ted who tries to bribe him into disclosing details of the layout. Bill refuses to hold any meetings with Ted so as to avoid suspicion, and instead informs Ted to look for further information, late at night, at an odd-looking wall he has started building. Perplexed, Ted follows instructions and is dismayed when he realizes what Bill wanted to say. What is the news?

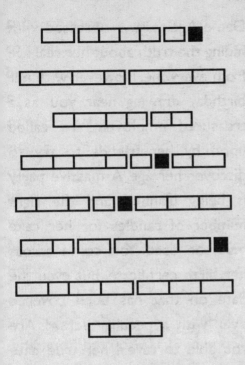

Brick bother

97

Candle kerfuffle

Dame Agelessia is obsessed with hiding the truth about her real age from everyone. However, with her birthday drawing near, you, as a treasured employee, are called upon by her friends to try to discover her age. A massive party is being planned, and the right number of candles for her cake must be used. You come across her birth certificate, but even the date on that has been covered over with a peculiar scrawl. Are you able to reveal her true date of birth?

Candle kerfuffle

⊙ ♎ ⚹ ☿ II

♄ ☿ ⚹ ♍ ♓ ✶

♌ ♀ ♌ ♌ ♅ ✶ ✶ ♌ ♌

♄ ♀ ♄ ✶ Y

♄ ♀ ♒ ♅

Absent astronaut

During a space mission, one of the astronauts mysteriously disappeared while walking on the moon. With much concern, the other astronauts went down to the surface to look for him after he failed to return to the ship when time was up. On reaching the surface of the moon, there was no sign of him but written in the dust was what seemed to be a coded message. Can you work out what happened to the missing astronaut?

B5 B4 A4 C3 A1 C5
C5 A5 A4 / A2 E4 /
D4 B3 A5 / A5 C3
A5 C2 E4

A1 C2 / C4 C3 /
D3 C5 A1 A3 A5 D3
B3 B4 C5 /A3 A1 C1
C1 A5 A4 / C2 E4
D1 D5 D2 /
D4 E2 C4

B3 A5 C1 C5

Absent astronaut

Cockroach conundrum

Jim Hill's parents had brought him all the way from LA to stay at a real English castle. It was a pain! No disco, no computer games, and no burgers. He thought he would die. Then he noticed something strange. The castle was full of odd-looking bugs. At first he thought they were some strange English bug but, when he looked closely, he could see that they were ordinary cockroaches that someone had decorated very delicately by hand. Take a look at one and see what you can make of it.

-.-. --- -.-. -.- .-. --- .- -.-. ....

.. ...

-... .-. .- .. -. ... .- .-. . -..- -.-. . .-.. .-.. . -. -

.... . .-.. .--. ...

Cockroach conundrum

Pecos perplexed

Pecos Pete is trying to find a gold mine left to him by his Uncle Josh. However, Josh was a canny old fellow and knew that the location of the mine might be discovered by others. He left directions in code hoping that Pete would be bright enough to follow them.

Pecos perplexed

Alien encounter

Chris is on a space mission, and lands on Mars. He finds himself surrounded by a group of three legged, green dwarflings. They attempt to converse with him, but when they realize Chris doesn't speak their language, they start to draw strange shapes in the dust ground. Just what are they trying to say?

Answer Number 83

Alien encounter

Answer Number 16

Sharp-eyed sleuth

Inspector Sharp was called to the scene of a murder. The victim, eccentric millionaire playboy Piers Short-Sightedly, was lying sprawled on his study floor stabbed through the heart. Among his possessions Sharp came across an address book. At first it looked of no particular interest but, as he looked closer he discovered that some of the numbers were not what they seemed.

Here is what he found:

9–19–21–19–16–5–3–
20–20–8–1–20–13–
25–23–9–6–5–23–1–
14–20–19–20–15–
11–9–12–12–13–5

Beautiful, brainy Susan McSleuth, one of the brightest young things at MI6, has attracted the amorous attentions of fellow agent Duncan Dudd. Susan suspects that Duncan is not quite marriage material but, to be sure, she sends him a coded message. If he can decode it he gets a date, if not she will know that he's as dud as he sounds.

Spurned spy

N	A	E	C	V	A	T	D	O	S
S	S	N	E	H	H	A	U	F	A
U	A	N	U	I	E	N	L	N	R
H	O	O	S	R	L	E	D	E	I
C	Y	N	N	E	S	C	V	T	W
E	O	A	S	Y	U	E	H	E	F
T	C	S	M	N	L	A	V	A	Y
U	Y	S	N	C	S	O	L	L	U
O	A	I	S	P	L	L	N	L	O
G	N	A	Y	N	I	O	D	C	I

A novel novel

Jeffrey Fletcher, the best-selling novelist, has a slight problem. His computer has gone on the blink and seems to be churning out rubbish. He is supposed to send the manuscript of his new book to the publisher tomorrow but what can he do? Look at a passage from the book. Maybe the computer hasn't gone quite as crazy as Jeffrey assumes.

Szy cght hr brth s
sh ntcd th drk
hrd mn sh hd sn
n th plc phts
stndng tsd hr hs.
Wht shld sh d?
Qckly sh rn t th
tlphn nd dlld th
mrgncy nmbr.

A novel novel

The conversation's flagging

Tim and Claire, two great friends, live opposite each other on a busy road, but have been banned from telephoning each other as the resulting phone bills have been massive. It's a real hassle for them to walk across the road as the traffic is so bad, so they decide to flag messages across to each other. Without the flags, life would be made very difficult for them. Tim sees Claire frantically waving to him one afternoon and rushes to the window to find out what she has to say. What is it that's so important?

The conversation's flagging

Dodgy door

Dave found himself trapped in a pitch-black cellar, the storeroom of a hotel whose lights had all failed. He managed to feel his way to the door, but was unable to remember the code needed to get out. However, since the hotel which was operating on a tight budget, often suffered from power failures, the code could be found embossed on some card near the door which only the staff were trained to understand. What were the words which, when typed into the keypad, would release him?

O⊏ΓN
/Γ/∧⊤

Tim buys a second-hand nature book and opens the cover expecting to see the name of the previous owner. Instead he finds a mass of trees carefully drawn out. After taking his book to school one day, the teacher claims to have known the previous owner. Can you work out who it was?

Nature's mysteries

Domino dilemma

To the amazement of astronomers the world over aliens finally made contact with Earth. Their transmission was at first incomprehensible. It looked more like a game of dominoes than a message. After some weeks of work they suddenly made a stunning discovery. It was not only comprehensible but it also contained a surprise no one could have predicted.

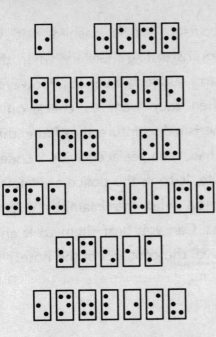

Domino dilemma

Bungling burglar

Security guards dashed out to Doomstead Art Gallery when the alarm suddenly rang out. However, when they went to check on a cherished sculpture, they found that it had been replaced with a coded note. It took the police a while to realize who the infamous culprit was. Can you beat them to it and reveal the contents of the note?

Bungling burglar

Fruitcake furore

For nearly fifty years Ethel Hodgkiss had been trying to get hold of her sister's secret fruitcake recipe. It became an obsession with her and she plotted countless ways to get her heart's desire. Eventually Vi, the sister, died and after the funeral the awful Ethel gleefully rifled through her things to find the precious formula. At last, to her delight, she discovered a cunningly coded note. When she was able to understand its meaning her glee was replaced by more sober reflections.

Sam Cody says, on reflection, this is a toughie. Read one whole column after another, starting halfway up.

G	D	N	I	P	L	D	I	N	A
U	L	A	U	I	E	A	S	I	M
O	U	H	R	C	W	B	A	F	E
H	O	R	F	E	U	V	W	F	R
T	W	U	Y	R	O	E	T	O	C
H	G	D	T	E	L	N	N	A	T
T	E	S	C	D	I	E	T	N	E
Y	T	O	A	I	H	W	H	D	D
O	Y	N	K	D	A	S	E	I	V
U	O	M	E	Y	V	I	C	S	I

Fruitcake furore

'Mayday' mission

You are a member of the space rescue team. After receiving a 'mayday' call from the spaceship Matrix 7 your team arrived to find the ship badly damaged and all the crew dead. In order to find out what happened, you consult the captain's log and the following message comes up on screen:

Answer Number 37

D3 B3 B4 C5 / A1 D4 D4 A1
A3 B5 A5 A4 / A2 E4 /
D3 C5 A1 A3 A5 / D4 A5 D2
D2 C4 D2 B4 D3 D4 D3

C3 C4 / B3 C4 C5 A5 /
B1 C4 D2 /
D5 D3 / A2 D5 D4 /
D4 B3 A5 B4 D2 / C3 A5 E3
D4 / D4 A1 D2 B2 A5 D4 / B4
D3 / D3 C5 A1 A3 A5 / D3 D4
A1 D4 B4 C4 C3 /
C3 A1 D2 B5 / B1 C4 D5 D2

D4 B3 A5 E4 / C2 D5 D3 D4 /
A2 A5 /
D3 D4 C4 C5 C5 A5 A4

Can you work out what the
message reads?

'Mayday' mission

123

Spot on

Chris went to see his friend Andy who had measles. He'd never had it himself so he stood at the end of the bed to commiserate. While they talked he started to look more closely at Andy's spotty face and, after a few minutes, he started to laugh so hard he had to run from the room. Andy's mom was totally perplexed. What can you make of the spots on his forehead?

Spot on

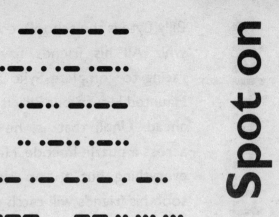

Computer crisis

Billy Byte is the school's computer whiz. All his friends have been racing to complete Syko and the Haunted House, but Billy is streets ahead. Until, that is, he comes across a puzzle in code. He's tried everything but to no avail and soon his friends will catch up with him. Can you help him solve the riddle?

Computer crisis

A-mazing message

Becky finds herself trapped in the middle of a huge maze, surrounded by hedges which seem to lead to nowhere. She discovers a pile of pebbles carefully arranged on the floor, and stoops down to study the pattern. She realizes it reveals the route to freedom. What must she do?

A-mazing message

129

Crew conundrum

Captain Stone has been pestered for weeks by young Ben Eager who wants to run away to sea. Stone is not your average pirate. He has brains, which is why he's never been caught. He expects his crew to have brains too. He decides to send Ben a message. If he cracks it he's in, if not he'll be left stranded.

A	V	E	S	A	T	M	I	D	N
E	F	O	R	T	H	E	S	O	I
L	D	J	O	I	N	M	Y	U	G
P	N	O	H	A	R	P	C	T	H
I	U	T	S	O	N	W	R	H	T
H	O	T	D	T	E	I	E	S	O
S	B	N	E	S	S	T	W	E	N
E	E	A	E	N	U	O	Y	A	T
H	D	W	U	O	Y	F	I	S	H
T	I	T	G	N	I	R	P	S	E

Answer Number 99

Captain Liftorf was carefully moving his private jet plane onto the runway, when an engineer rushed out in front of him, and started to signal an urgent message to him. Realizing the importance of this interruption, he slowed down to study the flags in detail and was horrified when he worked out what he had forgotten. What had he left in the hangar?

The problem's plane

Alchemist's almanac

At last, after years of searching, Magister Dominicus the alchemist has found the Philosopher's Stone! He is surrounded by jealous rivals who would stop at nothing to snatch his secret and so he decides to write it in the margins of his almanac in a cunningly constructed code. Can you work out what it is? The answer is worth its weight in gold!

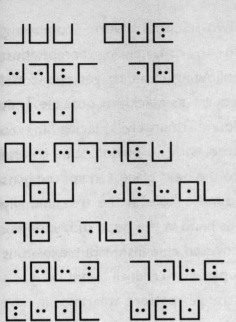

Alchemist's almanac

The hole answer

Two Scouts were competing in an orienteering competition, following clues to get round the course as quickly as possible. They found themselves facing an old tree, with no obvious clue to lead to the next place. One of the boys found a hole in the tree and slid his hand in the hope of finding the coveted clue inside. But, expecting a piece of card, all he found was a strange pattern marked in the hole, unreadable by being in such an obscure position. From that he found he was able to work out the next place on the route. Can you?

The hole answer

Safe keeping

Hans van Helsing, an Amsterdam diamond dealer, has a problem. He has just spent a fortune on a brand new guaranteed burglar-proof safe and now he has forgotten the combination. What to do? It is Christmas and the manufacturers have closed down for the holiday. He simply can't wait until New Year to get at his stock. He remembers that he has to press the buttons on the door and that alphabetical order comes into it somewhere. Can you help him break into his own safe?

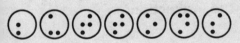

Safe keeping

Perplexing paths

The Trotter family are following trail through a forest, but instea of finding another arrow to lea the way, they find symbol inscribed on a tree. Simon, th eight-year-old, suddenly pipes u with what they have to do. What i the instruction?

Christine knows full well that her children will closely examine their own presents under the Christmas tree if they are labelled with their names, so she puts what the children think is a Christmas pattern on each one. In fact, they spell out each name. So which gift belongs to which child?

Puzzling presents

Kingly caper

King Arthur is just sitting down to a banquet with his knights when a carrier pigeon arrives bearing a message. Naturally it is in code. Merlin cheats and, using his magic powers, reveals the secret in seconds. You, however, will have to do it the hard way.

Sam Cody says: "The word 'castle' appears somewhere."

Kingly caper

Reel agony

Dave is a keen fisherman and spends all his spare time down by the river. One day he gets a shock. When he reels in his line it has been tied in a series of knots and hitches. Who could have done it? What could it mean? Each dot is a knot, and each dash is a hitch.

Reel agony

Bemusing blooms

The world famous plant nursery is developing new strains of plants. The problem is that they keep being stolen, so all the names of the plants have been written in code. Unfortunately, the head gardener has a terrible memory and cannot remember how to decipher the code! Can you help him to work out what these special plants are?

Answer Number 38

Sam Cody says: "Grid codes can work backward too, and it's not just I and J that can share a space."

1) E4 C4 E5 E3 C5 /
D2 B3 D2 B2

2) A1 E1 C4 C4 C1 A3 /
D4 E1 B3 E5 C2 D2 A5 C3

3) D4 C1 C4 E2 E1 C2 /
C4 E5 B3 C5 B2 B5 A5 B3

4) E4 C4 A5 E1 /
E3 D3 B3 A1 B2 E5 C2 B1
D3 E1 C3 A5 C3

5) C4 D2 C4 E5 E3 / C4 D2 C4 A1

Bemusing blooms

Nauseating numbers

Tom and David were halfway through a tough arithmetic exam when David noticed Tom holding up three fingers. Realizing that he wanted to know how to do question three, but also that the teachers present were on the lookout for any cheating, David scribbled a coded answer on some paper, hoping that if it was found, the teachers would be none the wiser. Tom picked up the paper dropped on the floor and studied it until all became clear. Just what did he have to do?

Nauseating numbers

Rainbow riddle

The famous explorer, Samuel Gardener, was in the wilds of Africa looking for the lost tombs of the Genmah people. While exploring a cave, he came across a door on which were symbols of Genmah origin. The door was locked. Also on the door was a rainbow pattern with letters written in each of the colored bands. These held the key to the secret door! Can you work out what it is?

Rainbow riddle

Shrewd Sean

To his surprise Sean O'Leary has inherited a castle in Ireland from an uncle he hardly knew. At first it seems a mixed blessing. The castle is beautiful but in need of expensive repairs that he could never afford. Then one day, quite by accident, he comes across an intriguing paper pinned to the wall in one of the outbuildings. At first he can make nothing of it but, just as he is about the give up, he sees his own name hidden among the words. A few minutes later his face is wreathed in smiles. Do you know why?

W	O	L	L	O	F	N	A	E	S
T	I	T	N	U	D	N	U	O	R
H	L	E	H	T	O	T	U	O	D
I	I	H	O	G	E	G	A	Y	N
S	T	E	L	E	H	D	S	S	A
W	E	A	D	R	E	E	S	D	D
I	V	R	B	U	R	I	E	A	N
N	E	T	O	F	M	Y	M	E	U
D	N	T	U	A	L	L	Y	L	O
I	N	G	S	P	I	R	A	L	R

Shrewd Sean

Answer Number 100

Tribal tension

A number of hungry African tribesmen found themselves huddled together on a ridge in the middle of a stretch of desolate wasteland, surrounded by vicious beasts. They saw a group from their tribe in the distance, so they decided to flag a message. What message persuaded the distant tribe to dash over?

Answer Number 91

Chloe decided to go for a walk in her village and, on her travels, she spotted a local football match going on. She decided to wander over and was interested in finding out who her local team were playing against. She asked a spectator who the other team was and was told to look at the crowd to find out. Just who were the opposition?

Football fun

Cave confusion

Fiona was exploring on holiday when she found herself deep within a cave. Trying to find her way out, she came across two possible tunnels to follow. Unable to decide which would lead to freedom, she started to inspect the rough wall between each route, and, with the help of her torch, found what she believed to be an ancient inscription. Upon closer study, she realized the danger one of the tunnels posed. Which route posed what danger?

Cave confusion

ᒪᒥᒥ–
ᒪᒥ∧ᗡ∨
–ᗤ
∖ᗤᒥᒥ∖
ᗩᗤᒥᗢ

Painter puzzle

Form 3B of Densely High School have been taken, kicking and screaming, to an art gallery. They show no interest in culture until Miss Smart shows them The Gamblers and explains that, though it is one of the most famous paintings in the world, nobody has ever known the identity of the artist. Jimmy Toogood examines the picture of some men playing dominoes in an old fashioned tavern with great interest and then suddenly announces:

"I know who done it, Miss," and sticks to his story in spite of threats of punishment. Does he really know? How did he find the name? The clue is in their game of dominoes.

Painter puzzle

Ape antics

It's been said that if you gave typewriters to a group of chimpanzees and they had unlimited paper and unlimited time they would, sooner or later, write the complete works of Shakespeare. But who will make the sandwiches? Never mind. Below you will see what one such group of simian playwrights achieved after a mere 12 million years. The words are all there but in the wrong order. However, we have given you the first letters of all the words in the correct order. Can you work out what they have written?

Answer Number 6

FRIENDS COUNTRYMEN
LEND ROMANS BURY TO ME
EARS YOUR COME I PRAISE
CAESAR NOT HIM TO THAT
EVIL THE LIVES MEN DO
THEM AFTER GOOD THE
INTERRED OFT IS BONES
THEIR WITH CAESAR WITH
LET BE IT SO

Ape antics

FRCLM
YEICT
BCNTP
HTETM
DLATT
GIOIW
TBSLI
BWC

A troublesome title

Sandra was working on her first novel, but wanted to keep the title a secret until all was complete. She had written it down in code to prevent herself from forgetting it, and other unwelcome eyes from seeing it. However, you accidentally find the code and are totally intrigued by what it could mean. Can you solve the mystery and work out the title?

A troublesome title

Numbered knocks

You have been imprisoned in the dungeons of Schloss Zweitenfrühstuck by the villainous Count Eisschrank. Why? How should I know? However, he does seem very annoyed with you. In fact I can tell you confidentially that a pair of concrete boots and an early morning swim in the lake have been discussed. But don't worry, suddenly you hear someone knocking on the wall of your cell. Could rescue be at hand? You will have to unravel the code to find out. Sounds like some sort of grid code to me. Here are the numbers of knocks.

Answer Number 2

1.3/3.4/4.5/3.1/
1.4/   5.2/1.5/
1.2/3.4/4.2/4.2/
3.4/5.2/   1.1/
1.3/4.5/3.5/
3.4/2.1/   4.3/
4.5/2.2/1.1/4.2

Numbered knocks

Dotty dilemma

The troop leader is at it again. This time he is going to test the St. Swithin's (Wednesdays) Scout troop to their limit. When the Scouts arrive for their meeting the hut is empty but a message is scrawled on the wall. It looks like Morse code but, wait a minute! There's something wrong. What can it be?

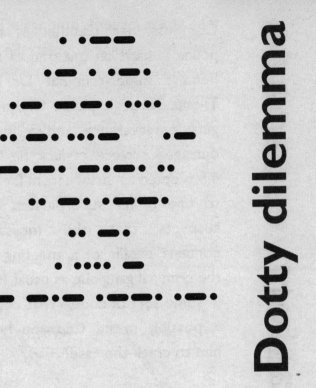

Dotty dilemma

Eastern escapade

Commissioner Gauden of the police is hard on the trail of the fiendish super-criminal Dr Ah Ti-Shu. Through pluck, fortitude, guts, perseverance and a most outrageous piece of luck he has intercepted a message from Dr Ah to one of his subordinates. He suspects that the message contains details of a meeting of the criminal gang but, as usual, it is in some sort of code. What could it possibly mean? Can you help him to crack the case?

Eastern escapade

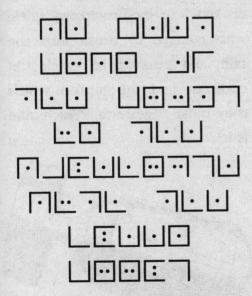

Button blast

The Evileyes are planning an invasion of Timidtown. They store the code which reveals which button on the control panel detonates their major bomb in a safe at the Evileye headquarters. However, these premises are broken into by Timidtown spies, who manage to break into the safe, and attempt to crack the code to find the button which they must deactivate. Which one is it?

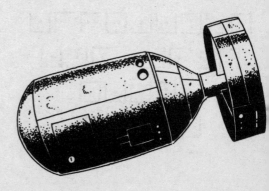

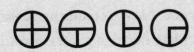

Button blast

Door dilemma

Castle Drak is a place of horror and dread once owned by the evil Count Vlad. But it conceals a treasure of such magnificence that many a young adventurer has dared to enter its gloomy portals in search of it. None has ever returned. Now yet another callow youth has decided to try his luck. Neville Duckworth wants to be a hero. His name is against him but he has courage, fortitude, intelligence and a lucky rabbit's foot. So far he has done really well and penetrated further than anyone before. Then he comes to the final test. He is faced by three doors and, above them, a coded message. What to do? He is pretty sure that to enter the wrong door

Answer Number 44

will mean instant death. Can you help him unlock the coded secret?

E	T	O	N	O	T	F	E	A	R
K	H	D	E	C	A	N	O	N	L
A	E	D	R	R	E	T	E	B	Y
T	S	N	U	C	T	O	F	O	U
H	E	A	S	E	H	F	B	D	N
T	C	R	A	S	E	M	Y	T	H
A	O	O	E	R	T	Y	E	S	O
P	N	O	E	P	L	O	R	O	L
S	D	D	R	A	L	F	E	S	U
U	O	L	I	W	O	O	T	E	T

Door dilemma

Battle break

During a battle between two rival villages, a soldier standing at the top of a castle starts to wave flags down to the opposition attacking from the ground. The enemy suddenly stop firing their arrows up as they acknowledge the message being relayed. What vital information stops the fighting going on?

Answer Number 47

Major Sneekly, head of the School for Spies, set his students this test as part of their final exam. It looks just like any other grid code but, to keep them on their mettle, he introduced a variation. Can you spot what it is?

Sam Cody says this is not half as difficult as it looks if you read left to right twice.

I	W	U	O	Y	E	E	N	L	L
R	E	V	E	D	C	N	U	O	Y
I	W	F	O	E	G	D	N	A	T
T	E	L	I	U	K	R	O	W	O
H	T	T	U	O	C	E	S	S	I
E	M	T	E	R	E	G	A	S	S
R	A	F	O	S	E	V	U	O	Y
T	I	D	A	H	B	Y	S	A	E
W	O	N	T	U	U	M	U	O	Y
R	O	W	T	S	D	R	A	H	K

Grid graduation

Dotty dog

A valuable pedigree Dalmatian is found dashing through town, creating havoc as it runs through the crowds. A young lad who's following the chase suggests to a policeman that they call the dog by its name to grab its attention. However, nobody seems to know it, until the same lad yells out a name and the dog arrives at a sudden unexpected standstill. What was the magic word?

Dotty dog

Lost legacy

Eccentric great uncle Silas passed away apparently without leaving a will. However, his solicitor, Giles Verry-Boaring, revealed that just before his death Silas sent him a note that appeared to be in code. He left instructions that all his relatives should be shown the note and allowed a chance to decode it. The first one to succeed in finding the will was to be the sole heir. Here is the note. Can you make someone rich? Remember, mighty oaks from little acorns grow!

LION (   ) OAKS

BEAD (   ) CAKE

BLOB (   ) OAKUM

COAL (   ) SEED

WAIT (   ) LILY

ARMY (   ) INDEX

MEEK (   ) SASH

Lost legacy

Lipstick to the rescue

Katy finds herself taken hostage by a couple of kidnappers eager to get their hands on her father's fortune. They let her out of the van in the middle of a dense forest while they go off to find their accomplices. Being tied to a wheel, she cannot go far, but manages to clamber onto the roof, and scrawls a message with a bright lipstick she finds lurking in her pocket. The kidnappers return none the wiser, and the journey continues until a helicopter passing overhead radios for help. What message provokes the call for action?

♑♍♈♑

♑♓♍♎

♓♂☿♑

♒☉☊

Lipstick to the rescue

Twain tangle

We're not even going to tell you what this one is about. However, if you look carefully you will find the names of two well-known young Americans who are in a spot of bother and need your help. Once you have found them the rest should be simple.

Twain tangle

T	O	W	Y	C	K	H	A	R	S
M	A	E	U	L	N	V	E	H	E
S	R	H	E	N	E	B	I	R	T
A	D	B	I	F	B	D	A	E	L
N	E	F	O	O	E	D	L	O	D
R	Y	U	R	O	T	L	E	C	B
R	N	E	U	N	L	H	A	N	Y
D	H	T	O	O	T	V	W	T	R
T	B	D	O	N	E	O	H	O	E
U	T	K	I	S	D	E	F	S	T

Party planning

Sinbad was organizing a surprise party for his sister, and was writing out invitations. Knowing that his sister would want to know what he was doing, he wrote them in code, declaring that he was working on some linguistic research. He sent the invitations out to family and friends – but when and where was the party to be held?

⊙ ◯ – Γ L

\ ◯ ⅃ ∧ L

\ ∧ – ∪ \

⅃ ∨ ⊂

∧ –

Γ l ⅂ ⊙ –

Party planning

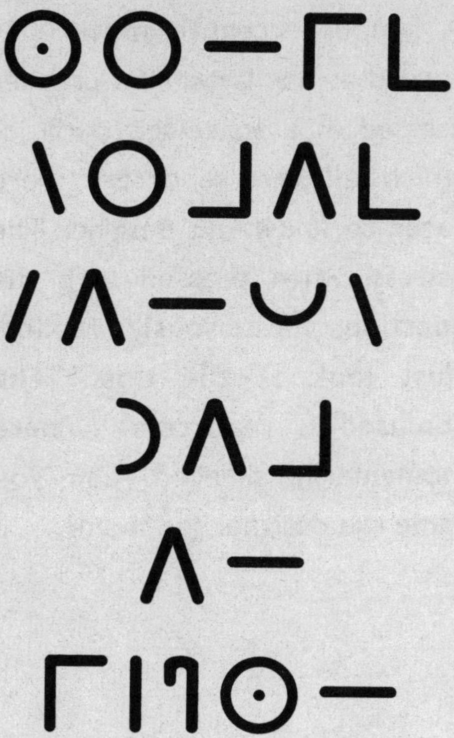

Designer difficulty

A famous eccentric movie star arrived at her latest film premier dressed in a space-age outfit of which all the reporters were eager to know the designer. The actress, when pressed with the question, mysteriously replied, "Just look at the dots." The confused reporters were momentarily silenced. Can you name the designer for them?

Designer difficulty

Moriarty in memoriam

Having finally killed off the infamous Professor Moriarty, Sherlock Holmes is taking a well-earned rest. While playing his violin in his study his peace is disturbed by a brick being hurled through his window. At first he takes this as a critical comment on the quality of his playing. But no! On closer inspection the brick is found to have a note attached to it written in some villainous code. Naturally the genius detective unravels the mystery in minutes. It may, however, take you slightly longer.

Moriarty in memoriam

Mixed Morse

Now here's a puzzle for you! The tireless leader of St. Swithin's (Wednesdays) Scout troop has arranged an initiative test. They are to travel cross country responding to instructions he flashes to them from afar with his torch. All goes well until he decides to really test their initiative with a dirty trick. Here is the message he sends. Can you work out what's gone wrong?

Mixed Morse

---- --- .---   -- -

- .-- .-. .   .--.

     - --.

.... .--. . ----

     - ---

--- .--. ... ---. .

     . .--

--. ... --- ---

     ... ---. .

--- .--- --. .   --

     ----. -

--- ... -- -

Literary loot

Chief Inspector Cornfield has had an anonymous tip-off that a major robbery is about to take place but he doesn't know when or where. A few hours later he receives a piece of paper in his mail. After looking at it for a while he suddenly rushes for the town library! Why? Here is what was written on the paper:

The arrangements
have been booked.
Everything you need
will be found inside:
38 28 E 22 6 1 8 38
E 24 36 A 16 6 50
4 38 E 1 40 1 6 0
46 40 12 0 E 24 A
40 A

Literary loot

Time travel

You are an assistant to an absent-minded professor who has just built a time machine. To prevent anyone from using it without his permission, he has written the instructions to start the machine in code. The time has now come to test it but unfortunately the professor has been taken ill and this is the only time for the next six months when a gap in time is available. The professor has therefore nominated you to try out the machine but forgot to tell you how to crack the code. Can you work out how to start the machine before the gap in time disappears?

Time travel

1.

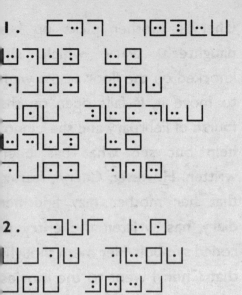

2.

3.

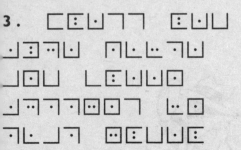

Diary dilemma

Cheryl's mother picks up her daughter's diary which she knocked on the floor as she went to move it. It falls open on the fourth of February, and she cannot help but see what has been written. However, Cheryl, fearing that her mother may find her diary, has written the entry in coded symbols. Her mom thought that Cheryl went to the movies with some friends on that evening but where did she really go?

Diary dilemma

Rocky revelation

A couple move into an old house and spend a day trying to sort out the garden. Helen uncovers a rock by the pond with what she believes to be an ancient inscription. Full of excitement, she takes it to the local museum where the expert on duty reveals that the rock is of no value whatsoever. When she asks why, the expert tells her the true meaning of the code. What is it?

Rocky revelation

Lost lyrics

Fading pop star Danny Devine had written a new song that he just knew would storm to the No. I spot and save his crumbling career. At first he had it scribbled on the back of an envelope but then he was suddenly afraid that someone would steal his idea. So he decided to throw away the envelope and write the lyrics in code in the inside of his guitar case. He had only got as far as the title when he was called away to answer the phone. When he came back his guitar case was gone! This is what he had written. Can you decode it?

Answer Number 13

Sam Cody reminds you that there are five vowels and you don't have to stop where you're told to!

2F3.L2.HT. N3.Y1.D1

Lost lyrics

Castle conundrum

Robin Hood has just received a strange message by carrier pigeon. Naturally he and his merry men are just itching to dash off <u>on</u> another swashbuckling adventure but where to? This looks like some sort of grid code, but how does it work?

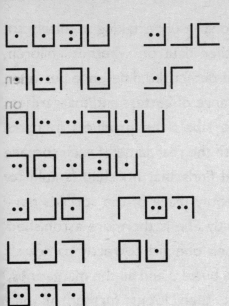

Castle conundrum

Spread survey

Shona is undertaking a survey to gather data on whether children can detect the difference between a range of butters and margarines. She labels the products in code with the real name of each spread, and finds that no child is able to identify many of the spreads correctly. She is therefore astonished when one girl correctly names all the butters and all the margarines, but then looks further at her answer sheet and finds symbols similar to those of the spreads drawn carefully at the top. What does the girl have to say?

Spread survey

Initially puzzling

Even very small changes to a message can help to conceal the meaning. Laura Lane is only six and hasn't been writing for very long but even so she worked out a way of turning a message into code. This is the caption she put on one of her drawings.

DHIS GS HY KOG DITTING DN FIS BOGHOUSE GITH S VONE.

What did she mean?

Initially puzzling

Mission complete

A relief mission was dropping essential food supplies over an isolated village suffering from a severe drought in the middle of nowhere. Being unable to land, and the crew having no knowledge of the native language, they scribbled a note on some paper in what they hoped was a language they would understand, knowing that blind people lived on the camp. The message was vital if the food was to be consumed safely. What must the natives do to some of the supplies to avoid illness?

Answer Number 105

ㄱ∪/−
ꓒ∩I∪ꓒ
Ⴑⅼ∧∧/
∩ⅼⴺⴺ

Mission complete

Time trouble

A young scientist finds herself trapped in a time machine in a distant century. She discovers that a password must be decoded to activate the time machine which has been installed so nobody else can use the machine. She's getting desperate to leave, but is having trouble finding the password. Can you help her out?

1   **Romans rumbled**
    Pax Vobiscum (Latin for 'Peace be with you'). The Roman letters that can also be used as numbers have been turned into Arabic numerals.

2   **Numbered knocks**
    'Could we borrow a cup of sugar'. What size do you take in concrete boots?

3   **Dad in danger**
    OVER MOON SEND BABY DADS KISS. The first and last letters of words in the left-hand column form the first and third letters of the new words. The first and third letters of words in the right-hand column form the second and fourth letters of the new words.

4   **Lost legacy**
    LOOK BACK (of) BOOK CASE WILL AMID MESS. Take the first and third letter of each word and put them into the brackets.

5   **Abducted astronaut**
    "Being taken to secret hideout in Santa Monica, LA." The alphabet is numbered from the middle. The odd numbers start at N (1) and go to Z (25). The even numbers start at M (2) and go to A (26).

Answers

6 Ape antics
Friends, Romans, Countrymen, lend me
your ears, I come to bury Caesar not to
praise him. The evil that men do lives
after them, the good is oft interred with
their bones, so let it be with Caesar.

7 Teacher torture
"I hate Latin. Let's meet after school
and go for a burger & cola." Start with
the I at the top right.

8 Muddled matrix
"Amsterdam, Frankfurt, Athens,
Karachi, Bangkok, Singapore, US." Start
at the A in the exact middle and go in a
clockwise direction.

9 Famous last words
"Look under the old oak tree in my garden." The words are written backwards
and every vowel is replaced with an X.

10 Initially puzzling
The first letter of each word is replaced
with a random letter. The message reads:
"This is my dog sitting in his doghouse
with a bone."

Answers

11 **A novel novel**
"Suzy caught her breath as she noticed the dark haired man she had seen in the police photos standing outside her house. What should she do? Quickly she ran to the telephone and dialed the emergency number." All the vowels have been removed.

12 **Image problem**
Dear Katie, Bet you thought this was from lover-boy Rick! Did you spend hours in eager anticipation? Sorry to disappoint you. It was only from your best friend in all the world (who you now hate), Rachel.
This is mirror writing. Katie guessed that whilst she was looking in the bathroom mirror to brush her teeth. Hold the page up to a mirror and you will see the answer.

13 **Lost lyrics**
"A Day in the Life" (sorry Danny, it's been done!). The words are spelled backwards and with numbers in place of the vowels. The full stops are there to fool you.

14 **Missing Magnus**
"Gone to South of France back Friday." The dashes are there to mislead.

Answers

15 **Computer crime**
"He has a new program almost finished.
I will send you details ASAP – Sam."
This substitution code works backwards
(i.e., 26 = A, 1 = Z).

16 **Sharp-eyed sleuth**
"I suspect that my wife wants to kill
me." This is a simple number code
(1 = A, Z = 26), and the only problem is
working out where to break up the
strings of numbers.

17 **Teacher's travels**
"I have been called away on urgent
business. Anyone who can decode this
may go home early." This is a simple
letter code: M = A, L = Z, etc.

18 **Et tu Brute?**
"We shall stab him in the Forum." This
is a simple letter code: J = A, I = Z, etc.

19 **Shakespeare shocker**
"Roses are red, violets are blue, I wrote
Shakespeare, phooey to you!"

20 **Gang greetings**
"You can join our gang as soon as you
can read this note."

Answers

21 **Pecos perplexed**
"From Dead Men's Gulch ride two hours north until you see a cactus shaped like a letter Y. The mine is one hundred paces east of there."

22 **Computer crisis**
"To open the secret passage Press Control C and Left Shift together."

23 **Kingly caper**
"Have been imprisoned in castle by very large ogre. Can you help? Yours faithfully, Princess Linsey."

24 **Eastern escapade**
"We meet down by the docks in the warehouse with the green doors."

25 **Moriarty in memoriam**
"Good try, Holmes, but I still live and will return."

26 **Castle conundrum**
"Held captive by wicked uncle. Can you get me out?" The message is from Maid Marian.

27 **Alchemist's almanac**
"Add mercury to the mixture and bring to the boil stirring frequently."

Answers

28 **Templar trouble**
"Ha ha. Caught you! Don't be so nosy!"

29 **Baffling bard**
"For never was a story of more woe
Than this of Juliet and her Romeo."

30 **Generation game**
"If you want a clue as to where I am
look in the pantry under the jam."

31 **Time travel**
1. Put solid fuel in tank one and liquid
   fuel in tank two.
2. Key in date time and location.
3. Press red blue white and green
   buttons in that order.

32 **Desert dilemma**
1) Death water
2) Killer drink
3) Water of life
4) Poisonous potion
(Therefore cask 3 is the safe one to
drink from.)

33 **Filmstar frights**
"Do not worry. Police have put their
plan into action and the culprit is about
to be caught."

34 **Bridging the gap**
1) Deadly drop
2) Safe and Secure
3) Plummet point
(Bridge number 2 is therefore the bridge to take.)

35 **Corruptive campaign**
Matt. Notes are on top floor of science block in locker on second row down and third from right. From Simon.

36 **Absent astronaut**
Kidnapped by the enemy. Am on spaceship called Myqur Two. Help!

37 **'Mayday' mission**
Ship attacked by space terrorists. No hope for us but their next target is space station Nark Four. They must be stopped.

38 **Bemusing blooms**
1) Black iris
2) Yellow geranium
3) Golden larkspur
4) Blue chrysanthemum
5) Lilac lily

Answers

39 **Party pooper**
"You can only come to my party if you are bright enough to follow the trail I have left for you. Come to my place Monday at seven." Just follow the trail from the bottom right corner.

40 **Strange last words**
"We are surrounded and badly outnumbered. Please send all available reinforcements as soon as possible – Colonel Strange." This is a zig-zag message.

41 **Spurned spy**
"I could only fall in love with a spy as clever and cunning as myself. So unless you can read this note you have no chance – Susan." This is a zig-zag message.

42 **Crew conundrum**
"The ship leaves at midnight on the spring tide. If you want to join my crew you need sharp wits – Stone." This is a spiral from the bottom left corner.

43 **Shrewd Sean**
"Sean – Follow this winding spiral round and round until it eventually leads you to the heart of my message – gold buried here." This is a spiral from the top right corner.

Answers

44 **Door dilemma**
"The secret of my treasure can only be found by those resolute to follow a perilous path. Take the second door and do not fear." This starts on line four, column six and follows winding path out.

45 **Twain tangle**
"Tom Sawyer and Huckleberry Finn have found the robbers' hideout but don't dare tell. Look in the old caves down by the forest." This is a zig-zag.

46 **Fruitcake furore**
"Thought you would get your hands on my fruitcake recipe, did you? Well, I have v. bad news. It was in the coffin and is cremated – Vi." Imagine this is a mirror, so read from halfway up, then from halfway down, starting at the left column.

47 **Grid graduation**
"You will need every ounce of wit and guile to work out this secret message. So far you've had it easy but now you must work hard." Read from row one column five to column one, then from column ten to column six.

48 **Scout cipher**
I will meet you by the pond near the old barn.

Answers

49 Bookham's blues
"...thought you'd never wake up. The murderer is the old lady in the red hat."

50 Much morsing
"Have secured Television station. Leader will make announcement in one hour."

51 Shipping shocker
SOS, SOS. This is Royal Yacht Britannia. Sinking fast. God save the Queen.

52 Dotty Dave
"I am Dotty Dave." The message is on the man's tie in Morse code.

53 Cockroach conundrum
"Prisoner in dungeons. Help." The pattern is on the bug's back.

54 Spot on
"Not really ill. Wanted to miss English test." The dots on Andy's face have been painted on.

55 Reel agony
We're fed up with this. Why don't you take up soccer? Kind regards from the fish.

56 **Dotty dilemma**
"We are having a picnic in the park."
The order of letters in each word is
changed.

57 **Mixed Morse**
You need to be a clever Scout to work
out what I've done. (The dots are
dashes, and the dashes are dots.)

58 **Domino dilemma**
I don't suppose any of you chaps speak
English, do you?

59 **Dotty digging**
Made in Brazil.

60 **Bun bonanza**
I am hiding upstairs.

61 **Crate clue**
They suspected trouble and ran. Will
report again ASAP.

62 **Safe keeping**
"In each word push buttons in order."

63 **Painter puzzle**
The dominoes on the table read: "By
Samuel Driscoll."

Answers

Answers

64 Catastrophic car park
A4, B5, C1, D2, E6, F3. The letters on registration plates are advanced by one from corresponding letters in each person's name. The numbers are A = 1, Z = 26 from corresponding letters in the name.

65 Literary loot
The book to look in is *A Tale of Two Cities* by Charles Dickens. The numbers give a message written backwards, with the vowels uncoded but the consonants are represented by a number that is double their alphabetic value.

66 Fishy Findings
"Treasure is buried in cave at base of Highsea Bay cliffs." Letters are replaced by the one before in the alphabet.

67 Rainbow riddle
Each band contains the name of a color. If you delete these letters the ones that are left give you the message. It reads: "To enter push three times on star."

68 Confusing cans
Baked beans.

69 Hidden treasure
The oak tree, Luckyhull.

Answers

70 **Bungling burglar**
The Boss strikes again!

71 **Nauseating numbers**
Five times the square of six.

72 **A troublesome title**
Red Alert.

73 **Lipstick to the rescue**
SOS stop this van!

74 **Rocky revelation**
Adam was here, May, Nineteen eighty-nine.

75 **Bolted boxes**
Mr Richkid's accounts.

76 **Candle Kerfuffle**
First of April, Nineteen fifty-five.

77 **Shopping strain**
Rosie's grammar book.

78 **Perplexing paths**
Follow the river.

79 **Button blast**
Red, third from left.

80 **Time trouble**
"Action stations."

Answers

81 **Hacker's horror**
Systems go.

82 **Wooden wonder**
Find a carpenter.

83 **Alien encounter**
Like a cup of tea?

84 **A-mazing message**
Keep turning left.

85 **Trunk test**
Dickens.

86 **Spread survey**
I know this too!

87 **Card clue**
B. Sotted.

88 **Brick bother**
The police are onto you. A long brick is
a Morse dash, a short one a Morse dot.

89 **Nature's mysteries**
C. Camore. A large tree is a Morse dash,
a small one is a Morse dot.

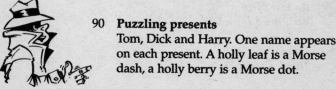

90 **Puzzling presents**
Tom, Dick and Harry. One name appears
on each present. A holly leaf is a Morse
dash, a holly berry is a Morse dot.

91 **Football fun**
Winnertown. A tall fan is a Morse dash, a short one is Morse dot.

92 **Diary dilemma**
Matt's party! A triangle pointing up is a Morse dash, one pointing down is a Morse dot.

93 **Nautical numbers**
Warning – iceberg looming. 1 is a Morse dash, 2 is a Morse dot.

94 **The test is yet to come**
Easter history test. ζ is a Morse dash, γ is a Morse dot.

95 **Dotty dog**
Blackie. The name is in Braille dots along the dog.

96 **Designer difficulty**
Spacini. Reading down the dress, the letters are spelled out in Braille dots.

97 **A rafty revelation**
It's behind you!

98 **The conversation's flagging**
We are moving.

99 **The problem's plane**
Left wing missing!

Answers

100 **Tribal tension**
Dinner's ready!

101 **Battle break**
Coffee time.

102 **Dodgy door**
Open sesame.

103 **The hole answer**
Forest waterfall.

104 **Cave confusion**
Left leads to sheer drop.

105 **Mission complete**
Must grind beans well.

106 **Party planning**
Hotel Royal, Saturday at eight.